REPORT

ON

EXPLORATIONS

IN

NEPAL AND TIBET

BY

EXPLORER M——H

(Season 1885-86),

PREPARED IN THE OFFICE OF THE TRIGONOMETRICAL BRANCH, SURVEY OF INDIA,
COLONEL C. T. HAIG, R.E., DEPUTY SURVEYOR GENERAL, IN CHARGE,

BY

Mr. C. WOOD, SURVEYOR, 1st GRADE,

AND PUBLISHED UNDER THE DIRECTION OF

LIEUT.-COLONEL H. R. THUILLIER, R.E.,

SURVEYOR GENERAL OF INDIA

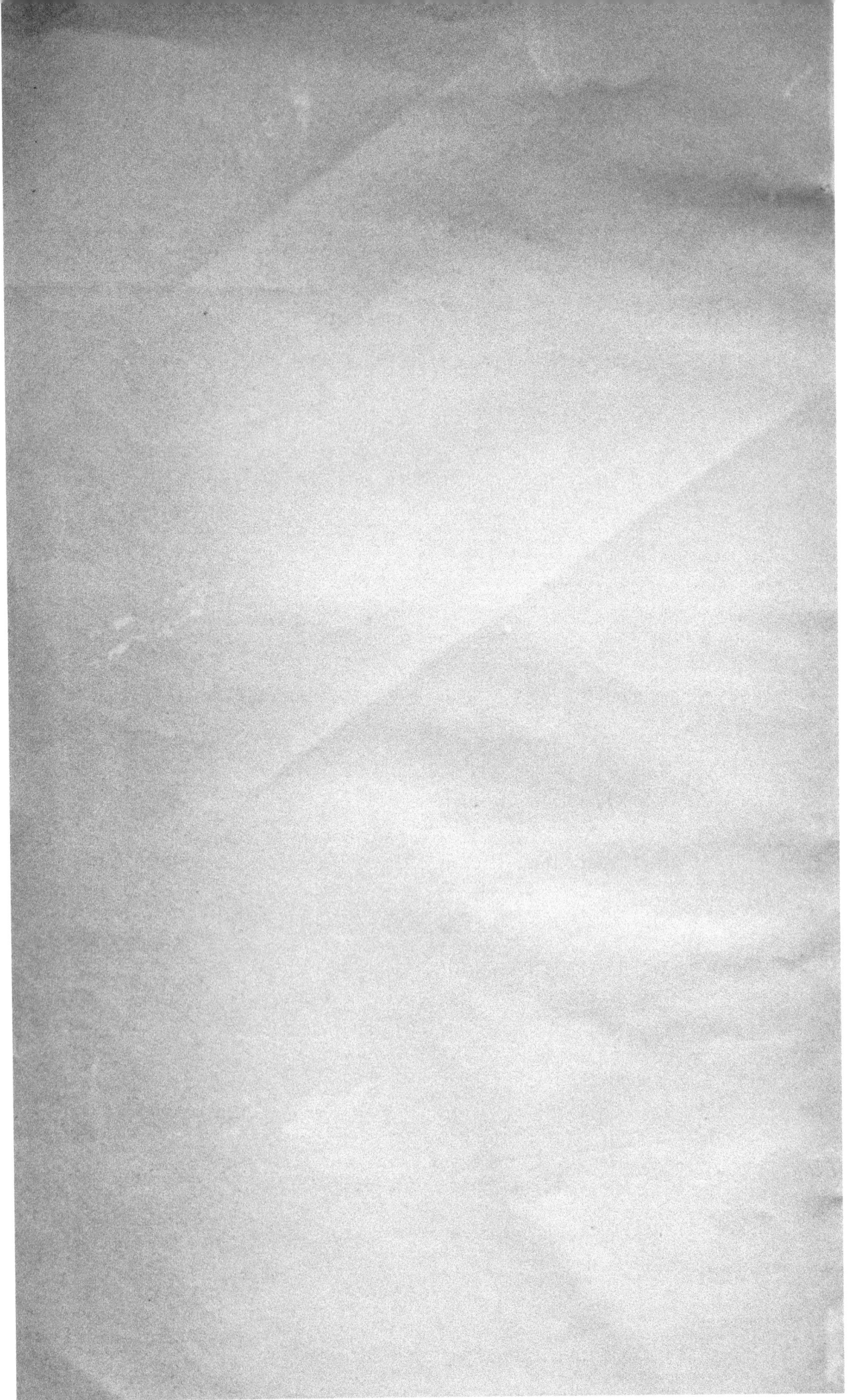

REPORT

ON

EXPLORATIONS

IN

NEPAL AND TIBET

BY

EXPLORER M—H

(Season 1885-86).

PREPARED IN THE OFFICE OF THE TRIGONOMETRICAL BRANCH, SURVEY OF INDIA,
COLONEL C. T. HAIG, R.E., DEPUTY SURVEYOR GENERAL, IN CHARGE.

BY

Mr. C. WOOD, SURVEYOR, 1st GRADE.

AND PUBLISHED UNDER THE DIRECTION OF
LIEUT.-COLONEL H. R. THUILLIER, R.E.,
SURVEYOR GENERAL OF INDIA.

Dehra Dun:

B. V. HUGHES.

1887.

PRICE ONE RUPEE.

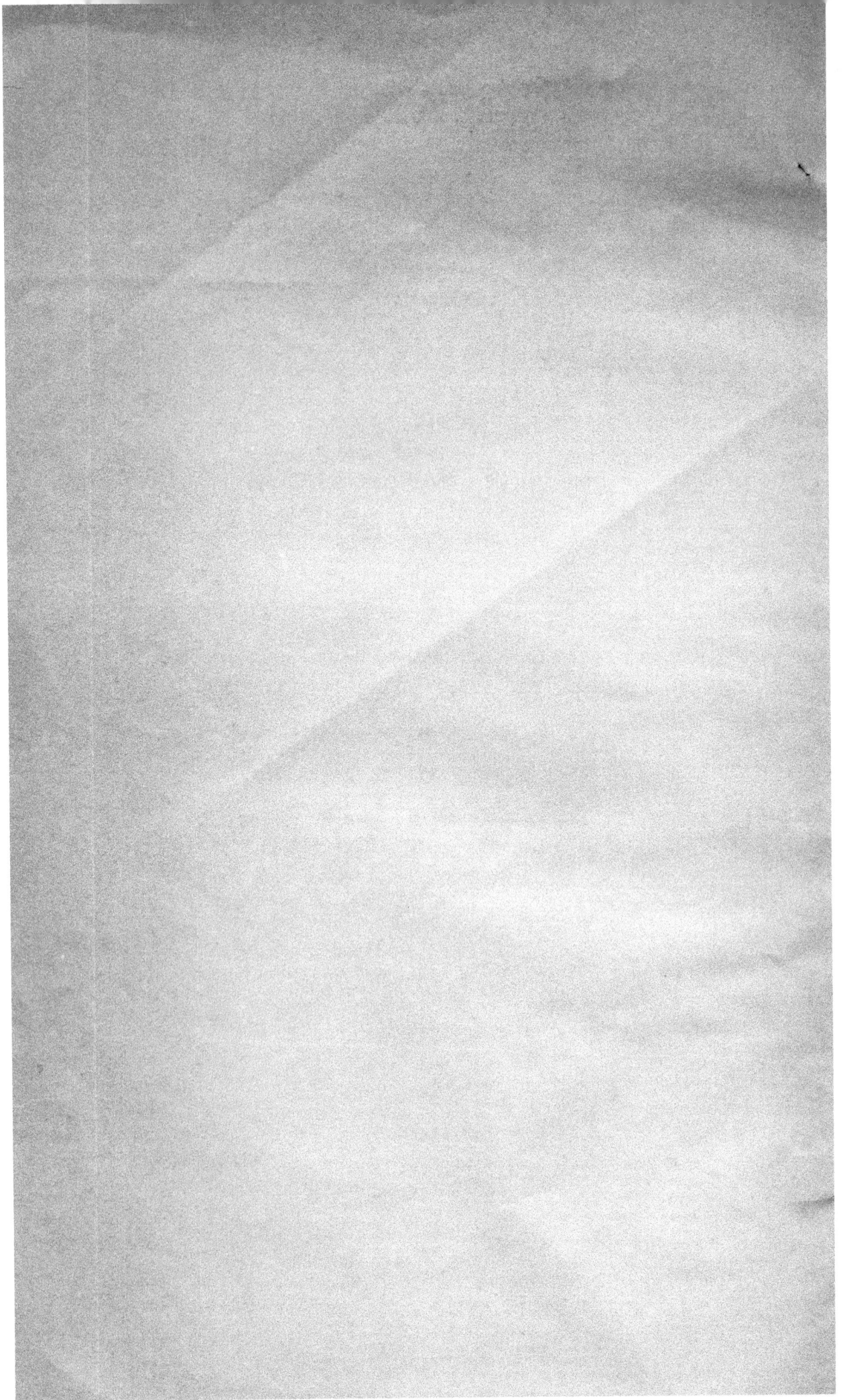

REPORT *on Routes by* EXPLORER M——H *from* (1) *Dagmára thána viá the Dúdhkosi and Pángula pass to Dingri in Tibet;* (2) *Dingri to Kirong viá Jongkhajong;* (3) *Kirong viá the Tirsúli river to Arughát on the Búri Gunduk;* (4) *Arughát to Nubri on the Búri Gunduk; and* (5) *Arughát viá the Búri Gunduk to Deoghát, and thence down the Naráini to Tirbeni: compiled in the Office of the Trigonometrical Branch, Survey of India, by* Mr. C. WOOD, *Surveyor, 1st Grade.*

The Explorer was directed to follow up the Dúdhkosi river and thence to reach Dingri*: he was then to turn westwards and find his way by Jongkhajong to Kirong* whence he was to travel further westwards till he reached Nubri (near the head-waters of the Búri Gunduk); and, following the course of that river, to return to India by Tirbenighát*. This programme he has succeeded in carrying out with a few unavoidable exceptions, but the want† of hypsometrical observations deprives his route of a place in the first rank of trans-frontier explorations. His route however traverses more than 420 miles of new ground, and, besides tracing the Dúdhkosi to its source, it fills the gap between Dingri—Jongkhajong—Kirong noticed as a desideratum on p. 4—b of Appendix to the Annual Report of the Great Trigonometrical Survey for 1871-72.

2. Having received orders on 12th April 1885 to arrange for his trip, the explorer went to Kumaun to engage companions and servants for the journey, and succeeded in engaging one man of Kumaun and three Dotiáls (Nepalese). He states that on his return to Almora he fell ill, and again at Kátgodám: he thus lost 2 months, and did not reach Durbhunga till 4th July, to which place two sets of boiling-point thermometers and a second prismatic compass had been sent to await his arrival. Unfortunately one of the boiling-point thermometers was found to have been broken in transit, and had he reported this by telegram a second one could easily have been sent: he however started with only the other boiling-point thermometer and it was not long before he had cause to regret his omission. As he was to travel in the disguise of a *baid* (physician) he here laid in a stock of European and native medicines, besides other articles suitable for presents to officials, &c. Leaving Durbhunga, he reached Jhanjharpur Railway Station on the 9th July, and thence made his way by road to Dagmára thána (in the Bhágalpur district) the origin of his work, situated about 3 miles south of the Nepal boundary.

Dagmára thána, *viá* the Dúdhkosi and Pángula pass, to Dingri.

3. 11th July.—Left Dagmára thána and, passing the Nepal boundary and several villages *en route*, arrived at *Bhagbatpur thána*. The thána is enclosed by a masonry wall, and holds about 250 Nepalese soldiers under the orders of a Colonel: on the west of the thána is the village of that name which contains about 200 houses. Distance about 9 miles; road good for carts; surrounding land well cultivated.

4. 12th July.—Having obtained a passport after making customary presents, the party proceeded on their way, and arrived at *Janoli* village, passing several villages *en route*. Distance 4½ miles; road &c. as on previous day.

5. 13th July.—At about 2 miles struck right bank of the Mohoriakhola‡, a gorge about 50 paces in width having water in its main channel to a depth of 1 foot; crossed and recrossed this stream several times till its source was reached at the Mohoria pass on the low range of that name which extends eastwards to Chaunria village distant about 5 miles west of the Koosee (Kosi). The stream flows away to the east from the point where it was struck. Went down the Bhajiakhola to *Mainagaon* a small village at junction of this stream with the Kamkhola. Distance about 6½ miles; road very rough, not fit for laden ponies.

6. 14th July.—Arrived about midday at Tirjuga village about 700 paces short of the right bank of the Tirjuga (or Tilju) river which is here about 50 paces wide with 3-feet depth of water. The road from Sinduliagarhí to Megzin (on the Koosee) passes through this village. When the river is swollen, small canoes, made of the trunk of the *semal* (*bombax heptaphyllum*) tree hollowed out, are used for crossing; the current being generally moderate. Tax on goods is levied at Tirjuga. The water being low, the Explorer's party forded the river and went on to *Asaria* village a little east of the junction of the Barukhola with the Tirjuga. Distance about 7 miles; road good from Mainagaon to the Tirjuga, but thereafter passes through dense jungle which affords good grazing ground in winter for the cattle of owners occupying the high lands to the north.

---

* Obligatory points previously well determined. † Even the few boiling-point observations brought back are worthless, as the bulb of the thermometer was not kept free from the bottom of the vessel in which the water was held. ‡ Khola = stream.

NOTE.—*The places where the party halted have been printed in this report in Italics; and the distances quoted are the horizontal measurements taken from the plot of the explorer's route.*

7. 15th July.—At about ⅜ of a mile crossed the Barukhola, a stream about 30 paces wide with 1 foot depth of water and taking its rise in the Mahábhárat range: followed this stream, crossing and recrossing it several times, for some 7 or 8 miles, and turning eastwards topped a spur and thence ascended to *Mahuabás* cattle-sheds about 2 miles higher up on the crest of the same spur. Distance 12½ miles; road very bad and steep.

8. 16th July.—Followed the crest of the same spur and halted at *Bámangaon* village on the south face of the hill below the crest. Distance 1½ miles; road very bad and steep.

9. 17th July.—Ascended to the Rautapokhri tarn in a hollow on ridge. This tarn is about 160 paces in length from east to west, and is said to be very deep: the water was very muddy when the explorer passed, but he was informed that it becomes clear in winter and that fish may then be seen in it. This place is held sacred by the inhabitants of Nepal, and in August large numbers of people resort to it for devotional purposes. From a point on the route 850 paces beyond Rauta-pokhri, the bearings of several peaks were taken, three of which have been identified with peaks trigonometrically fixed; the route then followed the crest of a spur emanating from Rauta pokhri for over a mile and descended along the southern face of a sub-spur, after which it turned to the N.E., and crossing the Rasiakhola stream (width of bed 50 paces, depth of water 2 feet) arrived at the small village of *Bhotiatár**, and halted there the next day. The Rasiakhola flows eastwards for about 8 or 9 miles and falls into the Sunkosi. Distance 6 miles; road bad except in the vicinity of Bhotiatár.

10. 19th July.—Crossed the Khárikhola, a small stream which falls into the Rasiakhola at about 700 yards E. of Bhotiatár village, and then ascended a spur to Bhojiabás village, after which several sub-spurs were crossed till *Yáribhanjang* was reached. There is no village here; but it is the resort of cattle owners who frequent the tract for the plentiful supply of grass which it affords. Distance 5½ miles; road rough.

11. 20th July.—Followed along the crest of a spur for about 5 miles to beyond Morenia village, and then by gentle descent to *Bijútár* village. Distance 10½ miles; road bad throughout.

12. 21st July.—Continued to descend for about 2 miles to Rámpurkhola, a small stream issuing from the spur at Morenia village and falling into the Yárikhola. At a short distance beyond, the large scattered village of Rámpur was reached: there is a chauki here, and the explorer's passport was examined, his goods searched, and a tax exacted from him. At about a couple of miles further, reached the right bank of the Yárikhola about 1 mile above its junction with the Sunkosi, and, passing the village of Jadanpur at the great bend in the Sunkosi, proceeded along the right bank of that river to the small village of *Chipútár*. At Chipútár the explorer was taxed again, and had to propitiate the official by making suitable presents. The road from Khatmandu to Dhankuta *via* the Sunkosi passes through Chipútár and Rámpur. Distance 9 miles; road good enough for laden ponies.

13. 22nd July.—Crossed the Sunkosi river by a ferry, and kept along the left bank for about 1½ miles. The explorer estimated the width of this river at 300 paces, and the depth at 12 or 14 feet; and as the river was swollen and the current strong, he had some difficulty in getting across. At about 2 miles topped the Halsiadánda spur (which runs from this point to the N.E. for several miles about parallel with the explorer's route at a distance of 3 or 4 miles) to the small village of *Jhábagaon*. Distance 4½ miles; road bad, not fit for laden ponies.

14. 23rd July.—Proceeded northwards and struck the Dúdhkosi opposite Khumbutár village; continued along its left bank to Jairámghát where after payment of a tax the river was crossed by a ferry. It was here about 50 paces wide, and had a depth of about 13 or 14 feet: the bed was rocky and the stream was a very noisy torrent. Fish are found and netted in plenty; and in places the signs of gold washing were met with though the explorer did not see the process in work. Continued along the right bank of the river, and halted for the night in a ruined hut. Distance 4½ miles; road very bad all along.

15. 24th July.—Followed a track parallel to the Dúdhkosi (which runs in a very tortuous course for a couple of miles) to Majhigaon a fishermen's village; ferried across the river to *Bilungtárghát* chauki through which the great military road from Khatmándu *via* Okhaldonga thána and Halsia Mahádeo temple (on the spur noticed under date the 22nd) passes on to Dhankuta. This temple is thought much of in the neighbourhood, and a free grant of land valued at Rs. 3,000 per annum has been assigned by the Nepal Government towards its support: the temple is annually visited in August by men from the surrounding country for the celebration of religious observances. At Bilungtárghát chauki the usual tax was levied on the explorer's goods. Distance 3 miles; road moderately level but too rough for ponies. [From Bilungtárghát the explorer detached his

---

* *Tár* = level ground on bank of river.

companion to traverse up to Hulsia Mahádeo temple. Distance 3½ miles; road good, and continues so as far as Bhojpur thána distant about 25 miles to the E.].

16. 25th July.—Followed a track along the left bank of the Dúdhkosi to some cattle-sheds situated near the point where this river is met by the Rákhola. This stream is here crossed by a wooden bridge 30 paces long, the depth of the water being about 7 or 8 feet: it waters an extensive valley which is highly cultivated on both banks of the stream and produces sufficient rice for export to the northernmost limits of Nepal. Distance 4 miles; road pretty good in parts, in others very rough. The explorer's boiling-point thermometer broke on this march owing to an awkward fall of one of his men in which the hollowed walking stick used for carrying the thermometer snapped.

17. 26th July.—Crossed the Rákhola and, ascending and descending spurs, reached *Lumri* village (of about 40 houses) about a mile below and east of Dumrigarhi fort. The fort has mud walls, and is occupied by 8 or 10 men, servants of the official who farms the revenues of the Rákhola patti. Distance 2½ miles; road too rough for ponies.

18. 27th July.—Proceeded about 2½ miles along the eastern face of the spur on which Dumrigarhi stands, and then ascended and went along it to the fort of *Asaliakhark*. Distance 4 miles; road bad in parts. A copper mine (now in operation) is distant about 8 or 9 miles W.N.W. of Asaliakhark. This fort is held by 400 Nepalese soldiers under a Captain whose duty it is to examine all passes brought by travellers from the south, and after full enquiry to grant fresh ones to those proceeding further north. The pass which the explorer obtained at Bhagbatpur thána entitled him to travel in Nepal: but as it was known that he intended proceeding northwards into Tibet, he was closely searched, interrogated, and directed to return by the way he came, the soldiers being ordered to keep him under surveillance for such time as he remained there. After a compulsory stay of 6 days, the explorer was able, by making suitable presents, to obtain permission to proceed, having persuaded the official to credit his statement that he and his party were inhabitants of Jumla and that they were anxious to return thither by Dingri, Jongkhajong, and Kágbeni, as being the most expeditious route.

19. 3rd August.—Traversed the crest and eastern side of the spur in a north-easterly direction, and then turned north-west, after which descended and, crossing the Dúdikhola, halted at the large village of *Lokhim*. Distance 8 miles; road bad throughout.

20. 4th August.—Crossed a sub-spur and descended to the Hungukhola, a considerable stream which rises in the snows about 15 miles to the N.E., and falls into the Dúdhkosi at about a mile below the point where the route struck it. The stream is 47 paces wide, and has 8 or 9 feet depth of water: it is spanned by a wooden bridge. Ascended another spur, and descended to the Yúkhukhola which comes from the same snows as the former stream and like it has a wooden bridge across it: its width however is only 30 paces and depth 7 or 8 feet. Halted for the night at *Chochim* village 300 paces to the right of the road. Distance 3½ miles; road very bad.

21. 5th August.—Proceeded parallel to the course of the Dúdhkosi, at about 1 mile distance from it, to *Waksa* village, the northern of two bearing the same name. Distance 2½ miles; road bad.

22. 6th August.—Kept pretty parallel to the Dúdhkosi, and, crossing three small streams from the N.E., halted at the scattered village of *Jubang* situated nearly 1½ miles E. of the junction of the Khumbu Chángbo (*Tib.*) or Bhotiakosi (*Nep.*) with the Dúdhkosi. The latter river rises in the Dúdhkund* lake (distant about 8 miles to the N.W. of the junction just referred to) which is said to be about 9 miles in circumference, and derives its name from the whitish (milky) appearance of its water. The lake is largely resorted to in August, both by the Nepalese and Tibetans, for the performance of religious ablutions &c. Snow-covered mountains were seen overhanging the western and northern sides of the lake. The hills on the western side of the Dúdhkosi from Waksa to Jubang are extensively cultivated; and large flocks of goats, sheep, and yaks find pasture on the slopes of the spurs which run eastwards to the river. Jubang is the first village where Tibetan inhabitants were met by the explorer, and beyond this no Nepalese were seen. At this village too the grass-covered huts of the south give place to shingle-roofed ones, and this style of roofing was exclusively found for some 30 miles to the north. Distance 3 miles; road not fit for ponies.

23. 7th August.—Followed track along western slope of a spur, and after crossing three streams and their intermediate spurs halted at a hamlet (consisting only of a couple of huts) called *Paia*. Snow-covered mountains were seen at about 5 miles to the east of this spot. Distance 7 miles; road very bad.

24. 8th August.—Crossed several streams, and passed through the large village of Chauriakhark† to the left bank of the Kusham Chángbo: this was crossed by a wooden bridge 27 paces long (depth of stream 4 feet), after which at about ¼ of mile the Khumbu Chángbo was reached.

---

* Called *Humichho* (= milky lake) by the Tibetans.   † *Khark* (Nep.) = *Dhong* (Tib.) = Cattle-shed.

This river is spanned by a wooden bridge 50 paces in length, the volume of water being about 16 paces in width and 7 or 8 feet in depth. Halted at the moderate-sized village of *Lobáng*, situated at 300 paces to the west of the route, from which place a pretty good road goes S.W. to Okhaldonga. Distance 6 miles; road bad as far as Chauriakhark, but practicable thereafter for laden yaks.

25. 9th and 10th August.—Proceeded for about 2 miles at a short distance from right bank of the Khumbu Chángbo, when being overtaken by a heavy fall of rain, the explorer's party had to call a halt for the night in a cave which opportunely offered a friendly shelter. Started next morning and crossed the Khumbu Chángbo at about ¾ mile, by a wooden bridge (about 30 paces long), a little beyond which the Lobáng Chángbo joins it. This latter takes its rise about 8 miles to the E. by S. in the Gumchho, a frozen lake of about 8 miles in circumference. After passing across a bridge over the Lobáng Chángbo, and two others at an angle of the river, ascended to *Nabjia* village. Distance 6 miles. This is the largest of twelve villages which comprise the Khumbu patti,* and is the chief resort of traders both from the north and south. The village consists of about 50 houses, and the inhabitants are more well-to-do than those of any village that the explorer passed through from Dagmára thána to Dingri. A little higher up than the first bridge at the angle in the river above referred to, is the confluence of the two main heads of the Khumbu Chángbo. These contain about an equal volume of water, and are named the Thámi Chángbo and the Pángu Chángbo. The former rises in a spring a little below a very deep lake about 12 miles to the N.N.W., and the latter at some 15 or 16 miles distance in the snow-clad mountains to the N.E. From the northern face of the southern watershed of the Pángu Chángbo, two or three small glaciers descend to some distance above the bed of the stream. Along the valley of the Pángu Chángbo, and over a main spur of the Himalayas there was till 30 years ago a fair road to the Arunkosi: but owing to an outbreak of virulent small-pox having been brought over from the east—which carried off a large number of the inhabitants of Khumbu—the road was closed, and it is now completely lost. From Nabjia northwards the valley of the Thámi Chángbo is very contracted. About 2 miles north of Nabjia and on a flat part of a spur, is Khumbujong, the residence of the Governor of the Khumbu district. This official is a Tibetan, and has held the post for the last 30 years: he receives no pay from the Nepal Government, but is allowed 15 per cent of the nett revenue of the district. The explorer was told that he pays an annual visit to Khatmándu.

26. The Governor for some time absolutely refused the party permission to proceed northwards by a route which he alleged had never till then been traversed by any Hindustani or Goorkha. The explorer had therefore to make a lengthened stay at this place, during which time he endeavoured to ingratiate himself with the inhabitants by treating their sick. One of the commonest diseases in the locality was goitre, and as he succeeded in curing the Governor's daughter-in-law of this he was naturally taken into favor, and secured the sympathies of her husband Sunnam Durje. This last-named individual was about starting on a trading expedition to the north, and by the exercise of sufficient tact was prevailed on to take the explorer's party in his train. The man eventually gained his father's tacit consent to the arrangement, and after a six-weeks' enforced inactivity the explorer again started on his way.

27. 22nd September.—There are a few villages in the valley for about 5 miles beyond Nabjia, but at Taran the last of them the limit of tree vegetation is reached, and the explorer had therefore to take 2 yak-loads of firewood with him before leaving Khumbujong. It may be mentioned here that from Jubang to Taran, barley and currants (black and red) are grown in tolerable plenty; but that south of this (with the exception of the Rákhola valley in which rice is grown as stated under date 25th July) down to the Mohoria pass (see 13th July) there is no crop other than Indian corn (*makai*): a little cotton is occasionally to be met with south of Asaliakhark. The explorer's party, having twice crossed the Thámi Chángbo by wooden bridges and passed Taran village, followed up the left bank of the stream and halted for the night in the open. Distance about 10 miles; road very bad above Taran village.

28. 23rd September.—After proceeding about a mile and wading across the Thámi Chángbo, the spring from which the stream issues was seen at a short distance to the east. A detour was made till the south-east end of the tarn (about 800 paces in length) was reached: the path then skirted the margin, and after leaving the N.W. edge ascended a narrow gorge for more than 2 miles to *Pángji dharmsála* (rest-house). The party first met a snow fall on this march, and for some days after had a rough time of it. From Pángji, at a distance of about 300 paces to the N.E., the famous deity Tákdeo (literally horse-god) can be seen standing on the summit of an inaccessible spur: it is a black rock, in shape like a horse and of about the proportions of an elephant. The explorer says that from the impracticability of the approaches to the spot, he is convinced that the Tákdeo is not an artificial production: the resemblance, however, he testifies to as being a perfect one. The place is considered very sacred by the Tibetans, and it is a necessary religious observance for the lamas of Lhása to repair to the locality once every 4 years and pay their respects to this deity. Out of deference to Tákdeo, no ponies are allowed on

* For signification see p. 19.

the route between Taran village on the south and Keprák village on the north of the pass. At Pángji the explorer came up with a large party of traders with their yâks on the way to Dingri, and he was glad of their company for the morrow when the pass was to be faced. Distance 10 miles; road very rocky and bad.

29. 24th September.—Starting at day-break, and feeling their way over the snowbed, which was extremely dangerous work owing to the numerous clefts met with—occasionally covered over with recently fallen snow—, the party after a toilsome ascent of 5 or 6 hours reached the summit of the pass. On the march from Pángji to the pass the gorge is extremely contracted, and large masses of rock brought down by snow-action from the heights on either side are to be met with in the valley poised like capitals on pillars of frozen snow about 30 or 40 feet in circumference and 20 to 30 feet in height. This phenomenon the explorer says he has nowhere else met with in his extensive travels over snow-clad districts. As to the pass he says it is decidedly the highest and the most formidable one he has ever crossed: he estimates the height at over 20,000 feet, and it is a very great pity that no accurate value of it is forthcoming. From about 8 to 10 miles N. and S. of the pass the explorer took bearings to a peak to the E. on the ridge which has been identified as Colonel Tanner's peak No. 42 the position and height of which have yet to be finally computed. The pass is named the Pángula: on it is erected the usual cairn of stones, with small flags stuck therein and the horns of goats and yâks laid over, so often met with on passes in Tibet. The ridge now forms the boundary between Tibet and Nepal. After a half-hour's halt on the pass, the party started northwards down a bed of snow lying in a narrow gorge, and as the sun's power was now taking effect on the fresh snow the passage proved extremely fatiguing; the gorge then widens and the water of the Keprákchhu becomes visible in a stream which comes down from the S.W. with another small one from the east: the explorer believes that the head-waters of this stream are at the pass, flowing under the snowbed he passed over. The route then runs parallel with the Keprákchhu and at a short distance above it along the snow-covered mountain-side to the east for some 3 miles till it reaches *Keprák* village and chauki: along this part the explorer saw the results of huge avalanches which had come down from both sides into the gorge, forming natural arcades here and there through which the sluggish stream of the Keprákchhu finds its way. Distance 12½ miles; road extremely difficult and dangerous. The *Gyángpa* (chief village official) of Keprák is subordinate to the *Daibung* (Provincial Governor) of Dingri; and he at first refused the explorer's party permission to proceed northwards, stating that any such concession would cost him his life: he however said that as the party had come in company with Sunnam Durje (the Khumbu governor's son), they would in deference to him be hospitably entertained pending a reference to the *Daibung*. On the fourth day, orders were received from Dingri forbidding the party to advance; but a little diplomacy gained the coöperation of the *Gyángpa* who next day with Sunnam Durje started for Dingri to wait on the *Daibung*. After some days, a messenger arrived to say that permission had been granted, and two days later the *Gyángpa* himself returned and arranged for a guide to accompany the party to Dingri. From Keprák there is a good route *viâ* Phalák (or Rungshár) and the Támbakosi valley to Sinduliagarhi. During the stay of the party at Keprák there was a good deal of rainy weather and very heavy falls of snow occurred on two days.

30. 8th October.—Starting from Keprák, the route continued along the mountain-side, with snow lying in parts, for about 5 miles, when it descended and crossed the Keprákchhu by a wooden bridge, about a mile beyond which it ascended again till the crest of the last spur (running nearly east and west) on this route was reached. North of the point where the Keprákchhu was crossed there is practically no snow on the mountains. Descending the northern face of the spur the party entered the grassy plain known as the Dingri maidán*, across which there is no path, but the traveller makes for a conspicuous flat-topped solitary hill which rising from a triangular base (about 3 miles round) attains a height of about 300 feet. The party stopped for the night about 3 miles short of the hill. Distance 16 miles; road good.

31. 9th October.—The isolated hill standing at some 400 paces to the west, was passed about 8 o'clock, and the party then proceeded, keeping in view the hill on which the Dingri fort stands. The town of *Dingri* at the base of the hill was reached in the afternoon, and the party occupied the hut which Sunnam Durje had secured for them. Distance 10 miles; road very good.

32. The town of Dingri consists of about 250 houses, and the inhabitants are chiefly Tibetans: there are, however, five houses belonging to Goorkhas and three or four to Chinamen who have established themselves at this place for trading purposes. The houses are all stone-built, a tenacious clay of a whitish color being used in place of mortar. The roofs are all flat; the larger timber consists of pine logs brought chiefly from Phalák and Nilam; on this lighter pine rafters are laid, which are superposed by a layer of strong furze locally called *dáma* found in large quantities in the neighbouring slopes; a layer of wet mud, from 4 to 8 inches in depth according to the calibre of the

---

* This is locally called Ghangár; by the Nepalese it is known as Tiglimaidán; while the Lhása people speak of it as Dhingri Ghangár (*Ghangár* in Tib. meaning plain).

supporting timber, is thrown over and well rammed. This affords a waterproof roof; but when the snow lays thick it has to be pushed off to prevent the timbers from sagging under its weight. The country immediately round Dingri is well cultivated, barley and pease being however the only produce. The inhabitants all appear well-to-do, but they seem to suffer a good deal from rheumatism caused no doubt by the intense cold in winter due to the altitude (13,860 feet) of the place and its proximity to the Phángju Chángbo (or Dingri Chángbo) river and the piercing winds which sweep over the plain. On the hill, which rises immediately from the north of the town to a height of about 300 feet, stands the stone-built fort which is occupied by the *Daibung* and 40 Chinese military officers who are in command of about 500 Tibetan soldiers. The *Daibung* is relieved once in 3 years, and during his tenure of office is allowed to trade within the limits of his province. There are said to be only three *Daibungs* in all under the Lhása Government: of these, one resides in Lhása, another in the Námchho district, and the third at Dingri. The authority of the last-mentioned extends from Shakia to the westernmost limits of Tibet, and he exercises both military and civil jurisdiction, short of capital punishment, within his territory. The trade in which the *Daibung* engages, so far as tea and salt are concerned, cannot be characterized as free: the former of these his servants and agents purchase in large quantities at Darchendo, and the latter in the Thok Jálung district. These articles, the men of the district are *compelled* to take over (in preference to purchasing from traders), giving, in return for the salt an equal weight of barley, and for the tea at 16 *naktángs* (a coin consisting of about equal parts of silver and copper, valued at a half-rupee) per brick (*dum*). The tea which the *Daibung* deals in is of the middling quality (known as *Chungja*) which can be had from traders at 8 *naktángs* per brick; and as each house in his jurisdiction is compelled to take one brick yearly from the *Daibung* at the rate fixed by him, he realizes a large annual revenue under this head. But as regards the salt, by taking over an equal weight of barley in exchange for it, he gains in seasons when corn is scarce, but loses when it is plentiful, for in the former the market value of corn to salt is 4 to 3 while in the latter it is 4 to 5 or 6 according to the season's yield. In addition to these two articles, he deals in blankets on the same footing as private traders.

33. The inhabitants are all Buddhists, whose social and religious customs &c. have been described in detail in the account of A—K's explorations and previous reports.

34. No gold is to be seen at Dingri; it is however much sought after, and as the explorer had gone there from the south many were the enquiries made of him as to whether he had any gold (or pearls or coral) to dispose of.

35. The climate must be very severe in winter, as it is said that the Dingri Chángbo is frozen over for 3 or 4 months. When the explorer was there, the Keprákchhu stream, which flows immediately to the east of the city and has a volume of water about 20 to 25 paces across and 1 foot depth, used to remain frozen till about 8 A.M.

36. The soldiers occupying the Dingri fort are armed with a sword, matchlock, and bow and arrows. The sword is the usual short straight weapon (in wooden scabbard) met with all over Tibet; the matchlocks are sent from Lhása; and the bows are made of bamboo which is brought in from Nepal. The soldiers manufacture their own powder on the spot. Lead is imported from Nepal and Darjeeling; but as the soldiers have no bullet-moulds they pour out the molten lead into a long hollow scoop in the ground, and then clip it into convenient-sized pieces which are hammered to suit the bores of their guns. They receive a small yearly pay (about 40 or 50 *naktángs, i.e.,* 20 to 25 Rs.), but they are allowed to engage in agriculture, trade, &c. They are drilled by their Chinese officers every week or so (sometimes on foot, at others mounted on ponies which they maintain for themselves), and there are periodic inspections by the *Daibung*. At these inspections, the soldiers always appear mounted in uniform and have to go through target practice. For the latter a disc of leather (1 foot in diameter) painted white is suspended to a rope stretched across two poles: each soldier in turn then rides full gallop across the field at about 15 feet from the target, and fires as he goes past: should he hit the mark, his officer who is in attendance with the *Daibung* scores a point. When all the soldiers have gone past in one direction, they return firing in the same way as they go past the target, to their original position. They next go through the same course using their bows and arrows instead of matchlocks. The *Daibung* then examines the notes of each officer, and for every point scored presents him with a *Khatág** after which the company is dismissed. The explorer was not much impressed with the marksmanship he saw, for not more than 50 or 60 khatágs represented the nett result of the shooting.

37. As Dingri is situated on the high-road from Lhása westwards, it is the constant resort of traders for whose convenience a *serai* capable of accommodating a couple of hundred men has

---

* *Khatágs* are small silken handkerchiefs, varying in size and value, which are brought from China and are extensively used throughout Tibet for presentation. Those given by the *Daibung* to the Chinese officers are of the cheapest kind valued at about 2 annas.

been built at about 500 paces to the north of the Dingri hill. The bulk of the goods is carried on mules, chiefly because they travel so much faster than either yâks or asses. A good burthen-mule (called *tíu*) is valued at about 70 or 80 Rs., while a good riding-animal (called *gyatíu*) costs five or six times as much.

38. *Trade.* In the part of the country traversed by the explorer from Bhágalpur to Dingri, the chief articles carried northwards are tobacco-leaf, cotton cloth, broadcloth, iron, brass and copper vessels, corals, and rupees which are used for making jewelry: for these the men of Khumbu go annually in parties to India—some even as far as Calcutta—taking with them muskpods, yâktails, antelope horns, blankets and stuffed *munál* and argus pheasants. A portion of the imports is disposed of in Khumbu, and the rest is taken on to Dingri. In addition to the foregoing, small quantities of salt and rice are imported from India, but these do not go much beyond the Mahábhárat range; also oil, which finds its way as far north as Khumbu.

39. From Dingri are exported into Nepal, Tibetan blankets, muskpods, goats, ponies, *ghee* (clarified butter) and yâktails. All the *pashm* which the tract yields is collected and bought up by the trading representative (*Jungchhongpan*) of the Lhása Government who goes every two or three years to Ladák for trading purposes.

40. *Produce.* The country northwards from the Mohoriakhola to Dingri (excepting the Rákhola valley which produces an abundant rice-crop) is extremely unproductive, the only grain grown being maize or Indian corn. Cotton is grown in small quantity as far north as Asaliakhark, and here and there in the southern parts a little *til* (sesamum) is to be seen.

41. Of domestic animals, buffaloes are to be met with as far as Asaliakhark; but fowls, pigs, and goats are bred and kept in every village as far north as Jubang. At Jubang and northwards are met large herds of yâks, *zobus* (cross-breed between yâk and cow), goats, and sheep of the long-horned species so largely used in Tibet for transport purposes. The yâk and the *zomu* (female of *zobu*) afford a plentiful supply of milk.

42. *Fauna.* South of Khumbu, Impeyan (*Lophophorus Impeyanus* or *munál*) and Argus (*Ceriornis satyra*) pheasants are met with in large numbers, and these are snared and shot by the villagers. Muskdeer (*Moschus moschiferus*), *thár* (*Hemitragus Jemblaicus*), and *gurral* (*Nemorhœdus goral*) are occasionally met with. In the neighbourhood of Khumbu, the Himalayan and Alpine choughs (*Fregilus Himalayanus* and *Pyrrhocorax Alpinus*) are to be seen in numbers. In the Dingri maidán, large herds of *kyángs* (*Equus hemionus* or *kyang*) and Tibetan antelopes (*Antilopus Hodgsonii*, called by the natives *cho*) may be seen roving at will: the latter are sometimes shot by the inhabitants; but with their indifferent guns the sportsmen's chances of success are poor. Flocks of wild pigeons and of the large raven (*Corvus corax* or *Tibetanus*) are found in the vicinity of Dingri.

43. *Flora.* On the Mohoria range (which corresponds to the Sewaliks of the western Himalayas) and in the valley to the north, the *sál* (*Shorea robusta*) grows luxuriantly: *toon* (*Cedrela toona*), *dhák* (*Butea frondosa*), *semal* (*Bombax heptaphyllum*) and *jámun* (? *Sizygium*) are also to be met with. On the Mahábhárat range, oaks, rhododendrons, mountain pear (*Pyrus variolosa* or *lanata*), cherry (*Cerasus padam*) and other denizens of a medium altitude grow in profusion. In the valley of the Sunkosi, the *sál* is again met, as also the tall bamboo, *pípal* (a species of *ficus*) and *semal*; but the trees grow sparsely in this locality. The mountain-sides from Dumri to Jubang are well wooded with oak, rhododendron, and occasionally fir, with an undergrowth of *ringál* (thin mountain-bamboo): and the higher elevations to the west of Jubang are densely covered with *deodiár* (*Pinus deodara*). From a few miles north of Jubang to Khumbujong, the lower parts of the mountain-sides are thickly wooded with a very large species of oak (probably *Quercus dilatata* called *riáns* by the Nepalese), birch (*Betula bhojpattra*), pine (*Abies Webbiana*, called *ráñdiár* by the natives, and corresponding in shape to the specimens of this magnificent tree met with in the Western Himalayas), and stunted rhododendron (either *anthopogon* or *lepidotum* which are known to attain the highest altitudes), with a dense undergrowth of *ringál* jungle: for 4 or 5 miles beyond Khumbu the pine may be seen skirting the bed of the river and the rhododendron for another 4 or 5 miles further up, with a few bushes of the Tibetan furze. After this, not a tree is to be seen, and till the suburbs of Dingri are reached the only vegetation met with is the short grass found in the maidán and the stunted furze on the hill sides. The furze met with is of three kinds, two of which are probably the *Caragana Gerardiana* and *versicolor*; the third is a thorny species of *Astragalus*: the leaves and legumes of all these furnish excellent fodder for smaller cattle.

44. The *Daibung* was away at Shikárjong when the explorer's party reached Dingri, and did not return till the 21st October. On the 22nd he was interviewed by the explorer accompanied by Sunnam Durje. The latter descanted somewhat too eloquently on the saintly qualities of his companion the holy Brahmin, and the *Daibung* grew suspicious that he must have been bribed to make so strong a case for a stranger. The explorer solemnly protested against having given any bribe, but declared that he had cured Sunnam's wife of a very bad goitre and had thus enlisted his

sympathies. The *Daibung* was evidently a man not difficult to persuade ; and the explorer, producing passports that had been granted to him in former years for trading in Nepal and Tibet, readily succeeded in convincing him that he was really an inhabitant of Jumla and begged permission to get home by the shortest possible route which was *viâ* Jongkhajong and Nubri. The *Daibung* declared that this route was absolutely closed to all but officials, traders going westwards and others being compelled either to take the southerly route *viâ* Nilam or the northerly one across the Brahmaputra through Dokthol (along the route traversed by Pundit Nain Singh in 1865-66). However, in consideration of Sunnam Durje offering to accompany the party as far as Jongkhajong and be answerable for their good behaviour, the *Daibung* on 24th October granted the desired permission ; and, ostensibly to afford assistance and protection but really to guard against the explorer changing his direction, he gave orders that from village to village a guide should escort the party and send back regular reports of the progress made.

Dingri, *viâ* Jongkhajong, Kirong, and Arughát, to Nubri and Tirbeni.

45. 25th October 1885.—Left Dingri at 7 A.M., and, passing Tokchhu village, at about 4½ miles reached the right bank of the Phángju Chángbo (the name of the Dingri Chángbo westwards of Dingri), and at about 2 miles onwards noticed that spurs coming down from the northern and southern ranges reached to within half a mile of the bed: passed Chhamda village where there is a chauki, and at a mile or so further on came to a hot spring* in a good-sized pool ; the water was too hot to allow of the hand being immersed in it, and had a sulphurous smell. The spring has a high reputation for being possessed of curative properties, and invalids suffering from rheumatism and other diseases come from long distances to avail themselves of its medicinal waters. Route kept parallel with the right bank of the river, and the party halted for the night at the small village of *Dákcho*. The villages on this march and on the route followed during the next two days to Makpáto grow luxuriant crops of barley†, pease‡, and turnips§, which were being reaped when the explorer passed through. The valley from Chhamda for about 25 miles onwards shows abundant signs of having once been very largely populated ; but it is said that in the last great war between the Nepalese and Tibetans most of the inhabitants were killed and the place now lies almost deserted. Distance 11⅓ miles ; road good throughout.

46. 26th October.—Continued alongside of the river passing Nilum‖ and Gunjo villages to the junction of the Phángju Chángbo with the Makpáto Chángbo ; forded the latter (which is only about 2 feet deep and about 15 paces wide) to the left bank whence a road leads northwards to Rákha Tházung Tarjum (on the route from Shigatze to Mánsarowar). Followed up the left bank of the river to the large village of Makpamau, and thence to *Puri* village. Distance 20 miles ; road good throughout.

47. 27th October.—Continued along the river as yesterday, and, passing the small villages of Sími and Tokchhu after which the valley became extremely contracted, reached *Makpáto*, a village of about 20 houses surrounded by a walled enclosure 10 or 12 feet in height. The *Gyángpa* of this place examines all passports. Distance 10 miles ; road good throughout.

48. 28th October.—Started before daybreak and continued along the left bank of the Makpáto Chángbo to the foot of the spur descending from the Lungola pass (snow-covered). Ascended the spur and noticed that the great Himalaya range to the south all the way from Dingri was well covered with snow. Descended and pushed on, from fear of robbers who infest this locality, through the Digurthanka plain to *Digur* village and post-chauki where a halt for the night was made. From Digur a winter-road leads down to Kirong. In the north of the Digurthanka plain, is the large village of Pungro, the residence of a rája. The plain, which on the east of Digur extends some 7 or 8 miles on both sides of the road, affords abundant pasturage for large herds of cattle, ponies, yáks, sheep, and goats, which are brought there to graze from so far north as the Dokthol province. The graziers (known as Dokpas¶) all dwell in black tents, and, in addition to their lawful calling, practise the vocation of robbers at which they are said to be adepts. A small party of them was sighted by the explorer, but on the discharge by him of a few shots they moved off. The spur bounding the Digurthanka plain to the north has a russet hue. Distance 26½ miles ; road good throughout.

49. 29th October.—At 3 miles reached the left bank of the Pungrochhu stream (which falls into the S.E. corner of the Pálguchho lake) and continued along it till it turns north-westwards ; after leaving it the party pushed on over a sandy tract to the S.W. corner of the lake where a halt was made for the night. The plain extended as yesterday to the south of the road, the Pálguchho lake occupying the ground to the north. The lake lies east and west and is about 9 miles across in

---

* *Chhuchhán* (Tib.)
† *Neh* (Tib.)　‡ *Táma* (Tib.)　§ *Libún* (Tib.)　‖ From here a bearing was observed to the Gela peak across the Brahmaputra which for the entire portion that was visible was covered with snow.　¶ *Dok* = black tent, *pa* = they of.

its longest part, the greatest width being estimated at 4 miles. The explorer was informed by his escort that this lake has no outlet; and so far as he could judge it appeared to be completely embayed by mountains, the spurs from the north descending to near its edge. The explorer asserts that there were no indications of the water having at any previous period occupied a sensibly higher level than it does, though of course signs were not wanting of the slightly increased height to which the water attains when its feeders are swollen by the melting of the surrounding snows in summer. The water is clear and sweet, and some small fish were seen in it. Distance 18 miles; road good throughout.

50. 30th October.—Shortly after starting entered a narrow gorge (whence a road leads northwards to Dókthol) and followed it up to the Chhárkiula pass, the last two miles being over snow. From the pass a snow-clad peak of considerable height (probably the Harkiang peak near Sarka Tarjum across the Brahmaputra) was observed to the N.N.W. at an estimated distance of 40 miles; in the valley below, to the N.N.E. and at a distance of about 2½ miles, a small lake 3 or 4 miles in circumference was seen, while further on in the same direction a range partially snow-covered, coming from the east, extended westwards past the direction of the peak just referred to. Descended westwards over the snow along a ravine, and then ascended a spur and proceeding along the crest again descended to the base where two watercourses met; crossed the northern watercourse and went along the right bank of the combined stream to *Jongkhajong*. Distance 20½ miles; road bad throughout.

51. The fort of Jongkhajong is situated at the junction of the Satu Chángbo (from the W.N.W.) and the stream from the E. along which the explorer travelled: it is about 400 paces square and is surrounded by a mud-and-stone wall about 5 feet thick and 20 to 25 feet in height with loop-holes all round. Along the interior of the fort wall and at a height of about 8 feet below its summit a landing is carried to serve as a foothold for the defenders. Two officials called *Jongpons* (Tib. = Governor of a district) reside here: they usually hold office for three years, and are relieved from Lhása. They exercise civil and judicial authority, short of capital punishment, in their district: this extends eastwards as far as Digur village; westwards and northwards for a distance of about 10 miles; and southwards for about 20 miles. Within the fort is a *Gonpa* (lamasery) which holds about 100 lamas. There are also some 15 or 20 shops belonging to *Newárs* (the trading sect in Nepal), and some 50 houses belonging to Tibetans: altogether, the explorer estimated the number of the inhabitants at 5 to 600. From Jongkhajong a road leads northwest to Tadum, and another westwards *viâ* the Satu Chángbo to Nubri. The country for about a mile or two to the north of Jongkhajong appeared well cultivated, and the inhabitants were reaping their harvest at the time. The *Jongpons* having examined the explorer's passport, in keeping therewith gave permission for the party to proceed to Nubri *viâ* the latter route: this however was reported to be closed by heavy falls of snow some way ahead. The party was therefore detained until the explorer, by making liberal presents, succeeded in ingratiating himself with these officials, who were eventually persuaded to exchange the original passport (which had been granted by the *Daibung* of Dingri) for another which would carry the party as far south as Kirong. At Jongkhajong the explorer took leave of his friend Suunam Durje but for whose friendly offices he feels sure he never could have got beyond Khumbu.

52. 3rd November.—Leaving Jongkhajong the route continued about parallel to the left bank of the Jongkha Chángbo, and at from ½ to 1 mile therefrom, till the post-station of Dámdoe was reached. The route then kept close to the river (which was crossed and recrossed on this day's march by wooden bridges) and, passing *en route* the post-stations of Hurma and Tashirák, the party halted for the night at *Gunda* post-station. The river flows through a very narrow gorge all the way from Damdoe and continues so till the hamlet of Rakma (about 9 miles above Kirong) is reached: no cultivation is to be met with all this way. The river at Gunda is about 20 paces wide with 2½ feet depth of water. Distance 17 miles; road pretty good.

53. 4th November.—Route lay along the river which was crossed and recrossed (by wooden bridges) several times passing Gunda hamlet (? Nain Sing's Sangda) till *Todáng* hamlet and post-house (on both sides of the river) was reached. From a little north of Todáng a glacier was seen between two spurs; and as the party was passing, an immense avalanche was hurled down with a tremendous reverberation loud enough, it is supposed by the explorer, to have been heard at Kirong. Distance 12½ miles; road as yesterday.

54. 5th November.—Continued along left bank of the river past a chauki (toll and post-house) and Rakma village (which lies on the *right* bank of the river in the angle formed by a stream from the north-west) to the large village of *Pángsing*. From about 300 paces before Pángsing was reached the snow-clad peaks of Gosáinthán and Dayabang were seen and observed to. Since leaving Jongkhajong cultivation was for the first time seen at Rakma; below this village the valley opens out to the east and is pretty extensively cultivated from about a mile north of Pángsing. At Pángsing, besides barley and turnips, potatoes are largely grown. On the mountain-sides west of the river two or three villages were seen. Distance 9½ miles; road good.

55. 6th November.—Proceeded parallel to the river, crossing a small stream from the north, to *Kirong*. Distance 3½ miles; road good. Kirong is a small scattered town*, larger than Jongkha-jong, and contains besides the houses of the agriculturists about 25 houses belonging to *Newárs* (Nepalese traders) It is the residence of two *Jongpons* who exercise joint jurisdiction within their district. The houses are all stone-built, gable-roofed, and shingle-covered†. Passports have to be delivered and renewed here, for which the party had to halt four days in consequence of one of the *Jongpons* being away at a medicinal hot spring distant about 2½ miles to the S.E. The view from Kirong is said by the explorer to be very contracted.

56. 11th November.—Continued in an easterly direction and ascended a spur on which a little tarn was met; then descended and fording across the Gundangchhu followed on to *Thungsia* hamlet. Distance 4½ miles; road good.

57. 12th November.—Continued parallel to the river, crossing a watercourse from the east, and halted at *Khimbuk* hamlet. Distance 4 miles; road difficult in parts.

58. 13th November.—Road kept parallel to the river and at about 300 paces above it till Paimanesa or Peingbhit chauki was reached where toll was levied and passports examined. Proceeded onwards a short distance till at a bend of the river the route nears it, and for about a hundred paces is carried over a gallery about 6 feet wide run along the perpendicular face of the rock at a height of from 15 to 20 feet above the water's edge. The gallery rests on thick iron bolts driven into the rock at distances of 5 or 6 feet, over which planking is loosely laid; the outer edge is fenced by a rudely-made rope passed round wooden posts which are fixed to the bolts. From this point the river flows in a contracted bed all the way down to Shábri. Continued along the left bank of the river to *Rasia*‡ (or *Rasua*) chauki. Distance 10 miles; road very difficult. This chauki belongs to Tibet, the boundary between which and Nepal is the mid-channel of a large stream (known as Rasiakhola or Lendichhu) which comes from the N.E. and falls into the Jongkha Chángbo at 300 paces below Rasia chauki: from the right bank of the river the boundary is continued up the mountains which run in a north-westerly direction.

59. 14th November.—Having crossed the Rasiakhola by a wooden bridge 45 paces across (the water-channel of the stream being only about 20 paces wide with an estimated depth of 5 or 6 feet), and proceeded about 100 paces further, the fort of Rasiagarhi was reached. This is a square stone-built fort with a side of between 3 and 4 hundred paces; the walls are about 10 or 12 feet thick at the base and rise to a height of about 10 feet, without any loop-holes. It is not garrisoned, but is looked upon merely as an outpost and is occupied by only some half a dozen Nepalese soldiers. Travellers are closely searched here, and those going south are passed on to Temuria Bhansár§. Leaving Rasiagarhi the party crossed a watercourse from the east, and passing through the hamlet of Biásiyári proceeded to Temuria Bhansár a village of 10 or 15 houses. Here the party was searched again and had to pay heavier taxes‖ than had been charged at any other place. The route continued alongside the river, which between Rasiagarhi and the point where the Tirsúli joins it is locally known as the Bhotiakosi, and passing the hamlet of Birda *en route* halted for the night in a cave in the hill side. At about a mile north of this halting place, the river is crossed by a wooden bridge over which a road leads to Pokhra *viá* the military post of Kuljung or Guljun. Distance 7½ miles; road pretty good.

60. 15th November.—Route followed close to left bank of the river (Bhotiakosi) past Ungul village to Shábru a large village situated at the confluence of the Shábru or Langdongkhola and the Bhotiakosi. Here passes are again examined and taxes (both capitation and on goods) levied. Crossed the Shábbrukhola by a wooden bridge 35 paces long (the depth of water here was 4 feet) and came to a sulphur mine which was being worked by a body of 50 Nepalese soldiers under a *Subadár*. A little beyond and close to the left bank of the Bhotiakosi river is a hot spring possessed of medicinal properties. The road here leaves the river which for a distance of about 20 miles flows at an average of a mile to the west. Passing about 200 paces to the west of the large village of Dunglang and through two villages named Bhárku, the road topped the end of a spur and then descended to the Tirsúli (here a stream 10 paces wide and 2 feet deep) which was crossed by a wooden bridge and the party halted for the night at the left bank. Distance 5 miles; road pretty good. The Tirsúli is said to rise from a lake named Dámodarkund distant some 10 miles in an easterly direction on a snow-clad spur: this lake is held sacred by the Nepalese who resort to it in large numbers in August for worship and religious ablution.

---

* Nain Sing was evidently wrong in stating that there was a fort here; he must have mistaken the lofty dwelling of one of the *Jongpons* for a fort.
  † This style of roof is not met further north than Rakma on this route, owing to the absence of wood.
  ‡ *Rasia* (Nep.) = boundary.
  § *Bhansár* (Nep.) = chief custom-house. ‖ Large traders of Nepal returning from Lhása are charged at Rs. 45 per man of their party irrespective of the value of their goods: Nepalese officials returning from Lhása are charged at Rs. 25 per man: and petty traders at Rs. 15 per man. The explorer's party was assessed under the last class.

61. 16th November.—Crossed a spur on which a little east of the route is the small village of Dhonju, and further on some streams from the S.E, then topped the end of a spur to *Thándi* (? Tangu of Nain Sing) village. Distance 4 miles; road good.

62. 17th November.—Continued the route past Gurang, the large village of Rámcha and several smaller ones to the village of Betráwati (at the angle formed by the junction of the Betráwati nadi with the Tirsúli) consisting of some 30 or 40 houses chiefly belonging to petty traders in grain and cloth. The route then kept near the left bank of the Tirsúli river past Simri village to the west of Naiakot where it turned westwards and crossed the river by a wooden bridge to *Khinchak bazár* (Kinchut bazar of Nain Sing). Distance 13½ miles; road good. Khinchak bazár is about 500 paces in length lying east and west, and the miscellaneous dealers all seem to be well-to-do; the trade consisting of grain, cotton and woollen cloths, metal vessels, shoes &c. The houses are all stone-built and roofed with tiles. At this place as well as on the opposite bank of the river, passes are strictly examined and tax levied on goods.

63. 18th November.—After proceeding about a mile the left bank of the Sámrikhola was struck, and the route thence continued along its sandy banks crossing backwards and forwards and passing *en route* two streams from the north. Halted at *Kákni pawa**. Distance 4 miles; road good.

64. 19th November.—Followed up the Sámrikhola as yesterday, and then by a gentle ascent to Sámri pawa at the pass on the long spur running N. and S. which here forms the watershed between the Tirsúli and the Búri Gunduk. On the pass, in addition to the rest-house there are three shops where provisions are kept for the convenience of travellers. Continued by a stiff descent till the Patharkhola was reached; this was crossed three times, after which passing 3 or 4 shops the left bank of the Baringkhola was struck: the latter is a good-sized stream coming from the N. and is crossed by a wooden bridge. Beyond this the road followed up a gentle ascent of about ¾ of a mile to Thárku pawa situated on the crest of a spur, whence it descended to *Bhagtani pawa*. Distance 7¾ miles; road good.

65. 20th November.—Ascended a spur and continued along its crest for some distance after which the road descends to the large village of Katonjia. Beyond this, after crossing a small stream and a spur, the small village of Charangia was reached, and at about ½ a mile further is Charangia-phedi† pawa. Continued onwards and halted at the small village of *Achania*. Distance 7 miles; road good.

66. 21st November.—At about a mile struck the left bank of the principal head of the Akho river which rises a long way off to the north and here takes a turn to the west. Continued along the right bank of the river passing the small villages of Belghári and Suporia to Saliánbiási†; after this the road runs at nearly 500 yards to the north of the river and at about 1½ miles from the last named village crosses the Hikukhola. The road then turns northwards and by a gentle ascent of about ½ a mile along the eastern face reaches the summit of the Saliántár plateau, whence it runs on the flat top and, passing a dharmsála at about ½ a mile, is continued to past the large village of *Saliántár*. Distance 7½ miles; road good. The country on both flanks of the road from Khinchak bazár to Saliántár is well cultivated, and numerous villages were seen dotting the hill sides all along. The plateau of Saliántár, which is about 5 miles in length (north to south) and nearly 2 miles at its greatest width, is elevated about 700 feet above the Akho and Búri Gunduk rivers. The ascent from the eastern side is easy, but on the western side the face stands like a mural precipice over-hanging the Búri Gunduk except where a passage to the river has been made along a flight of stone steps carried down from a distance of about a quarter of a mile. The plateau is well inhabited, and though it is not watered the soil yields a very good rainy-season crop.

67. 23rd November.—Having halted on the 22nd at Saliántár, the journey was resumed on the following day, and after proceeding for nearly a quarter of a mile along the plateau a descent of some 900 paces was made and the route then turned a little westwards so as to approach the left bank of the Búri Gunduk along which it continued till near the end of this day's march. At about 2 miles from the descent and on the bank of the Búri Gunduk is a brick-built temple where an annual religious fair is held in October: and further on the villages of Odári and Pipri were passed beyond which is the large village of *Lodánda* (consisting of about 50 houses enclosed by a stone wall) where a halt was made. Distance 7 miles; road good.

68. 24th November.—From between Pipri and Lodánda the river takes a bend to the west: the route however avoids this bend (being about 1½ miles E. of it at the angle), and going over the ground which slopes down from the mountains on the east passes through five hamlets and again strikes the left bank of the Búri Gunduk. The river was crossed by a temporary wooden bridge, and the route continued along the right bank. Halted at the hamlet of *Lábubiási*. Distance 6½ miles; road good for the first half, after which it becomes very difficult and absolutely impracticable for any but foot-passengers. From Mánbiási a summer and wet-season route strikes up the

_____
* *Pawa* (Nep.) signifies rest-house.   † *Biási* and *Phedi* (Nep.) signify winter-residence.

hill-side to the east and continues along it for some 10 or 12 miles: it then crosses the Búri Gunduk by the masonry bridge over which the road from Pokhra to Kuljung is carried, and keeps along the mountain-sides till it reaches the large village of Birjam about 20 miles further north. This route is only practicable for the smaller beasts of burden, viz., goats and sheep.

69. 25th November.—The route kept along the right bank of the Búri Gunduk, through dense jungle to *Khorlangbiási* the winter-residence of the inhabitants of Khorlang a village in the mountains some distance to the N.W. Distance 5 miles; road very difficult.

70. 26th November.—Crossed the Búri Gunduk at about a mile by a temporary wooden bridge and continued along the left bank for some six or seven miles when the river was recrossed and the party halted at a hamlet where there is a chauki. Here 5 Nepalese soldiers and a tax-collector are stationed. About midway on this day's march the road from Pokhra to Kuljung running east and west was passed. Distance 6½ miles; road very difficult and all the way through jungle. At about 2 miles S. of the chauki a glacier was visible to the east, from the foot of which a good-sized waterfall issues and plunges down a mural precipice of which the explorer estimated the height as 2,000 feet: for about half way down the water is visible in a connected body, but thereafter it descends as a shower of fine spray to the depths below.

71. 28th November.—Detained at the chauki on the 27th, and resumed the journey on the following day. The route after crossing a stream from the west is carried along a narrow gallery (supported on wooden beams) for about 800 paces: this is practicable only for foot-passengers and the smaller beasts of burden. It then kept practically parallel to the river and passing three hamlets on the way, which are the first villages on this route that are exclusively inhabited by Tibetans, the party halted at the large village of *Pángsing* distant about one-third of a mile to the west of Búri Gunduk. Distance 6½ miles; road very difficult through grass and underwood. From about 1½ miles south of Pángsing a summer and wet-season route strikes up to the east past Phiring village, and keeps along the mountain-side going northwards till it meets the direct route from Gunda (on the Jongkha Chángbo) to Nubri. Another route leaves Pángsing for the iron mines which are said to be about 5 or 6 miles to the N.W.

72. 29th November.—From ½ mile N. of Pángsing a snowy peak (No. XXVII) was observed; and at a little further on the route crosses the Dhunga Sáñgúñkhola over a natural bridge formed by two huge rocks which abut against each other at a height of 40 feet above the water-level. From the bridge a lofty snowy peak (No. XXX) was observed distant about 15 or 16 miles. The route continues west of the river to the small village of Niák, about a mile S.W. of the confluence of the Búri Gunduk and the Shiárkhola which latter brings down a considerable body of water from the N.E. At 700 paces beyond Niák snowy peak No. XXVII was again observed; and from a little further the route continued parallel to and at about half a mile above the Búri Gunduk which for about 4 miles above the junction of the Shiárkhola flows through a very contracted gorge. Halted at the edge of a small stream flowing from the S.W. Distance 5½ miles; road very difficult and through jungle.

73. 30th November.—At about a mile the route crossed over to the left bank of the river to the village of Ránágaon, and then kept along it for about 4 miles passing through the village of Bhúdgaon: the river was then recrossed and the route continued parallel to it, the party halting at the village of *Birjam* situated at about 400 paces above the river. Distance 8 miles; road for the most part difficult.

74. Birjam is the Nepalese name of the village which by the Tibetans is known as Nubri. It is the head-quarters of the governor of the Nubri *iláka* which extends for about 50 miles in length from north to south, i.e., from the Nepal-Tibet boundary southwards to about 7 or 8 miles north of Saliántár. Between Birjam and Niák the sites of several villages were passed which are occupied by the villagers of the neighbouring mountains in winter.

75. The explorer having reached the northern limit of his route in this locality, retraced his steps along the Búri Gunduk, and in six days arrived at *Arughát* on the right bank of the river opposite to Saliántár. The Búri Gunduk between Saliántár and Arughát is spanned by a wooden bridge 35 paces in length and elevated about 25 or 30 feet above the water level. Arughát is a village consisting of about 15 houses belonging to petty traders: a tax-collector also resides here, and at the time the party passed through there were 8 or 10 Nepalese soldiers at the place. From Arughát a good road leads westwards to Goorkha Darwár. At Arughát the party was detained three days, pending the result of enquiries as to where they had come from and for what purpose. The explorer professed to have gone all the way to Nubri in search of one of his dependants who he alleged had ran away from his home in Jumla with a large sum of money some time before, but whom he had not succeeded in finding. He said that having failed in his object, he was anxious to return home *viâ* Tirbeni where he intended going through the customary religious observances.

EXPLORATION REPORT ON ROUTES BY EXPLORER M——H.

He was then allowed to proceed, but warned that, owing to the disturbed state of the country consequent on the recent insurrection in Khatmandu, he was liable to detention in several places.

76. 10th December.—The route kept near the right bank of the river at first; it then ascended a couple of low spurs and descended to the chauki and small fishing-village of Borlangghát where ferry-boats carry passengers across the Búri Gunduk. The river lower down has a somewhat tortuous course: this the route avoided, and passing through the Májátár cattle-sheds the party at the *Sátbisitár* cattle-sheds. Distance 5½ miles; road fair, but rocky.

77. 11th December.—Proceeded along the right bank, past the small fishing-village of Baktárghát (where a ferry-boat plies) to the *Kundutár* cattle-sheds. Distance 5 miles; road as yesterday.

78. 12th December.—Continued along the right bank, past the Darguntár cattle-sheds to the hamlet and chauki opposite the point where the Tirsúli river falls into the Búri Gunduk. Distance 5 miles; road fair, through tall grass. The explorer estimated that the body of water brought down by the Tirsúli was somewhat in excess of that by the Búri Gunduk, also that the current of the former was more rapid than that of the latter. The hamlet of Páwátár, where there is a rest-house, is on the opposite side on the south bank of the Tirsúli and a road leads thence to Khatmandu. The party was detained here for five days, pending their ability to find security for their good behaviour further on. At length one of the petty traders in the neighbourhood, after receiving a gratification, offered the necessary security and the party was permitted to proceed. From Arughát to the junction of the Tirsúli, there are numerous villages on the hill-sides east and west of the river, but the low ground is occupied only in winter by cattle owners who drive down their herds partly to avoid the cold but chiefly for the abundant pasture which is to be found on the river banks. In several places on the river bank the explorer saw traces of gold-washing having been carried on.

79. 18th December.—Crossed the river, which is henceforward known as the Tirsúli, by a ferry-boat, and halted at the moderate-sized village of *Bichráltár*. Distance 1 mile; road good.

80. 19th December.—Topped a low spur and followed the left bank of the Tirsúli to *Phachchamtár* chauki. Distance 3½ miles; road good. The explorer saw gold-washing being carried on at this place by the inhabitants of Phachcham a large village on the hill-side distant about half a mile to the south. The party was detained two days at the chauki.

81. 22nd December.—Proceeded to *Hugdi* chauki. Distance 2 miles; road good. Detained one day.

82. 24th December.—Forded the Hugdikhola and ascended along the crest of a spur to *Jogimára* a village of 10 or 12 houses. Distance 2½ miles; road steep.

83. 25th December.—Continued along the crest of the spur to the ruined fort of Jogimára, the site of which is occupied by a hamlet of six or seven houses; thence descended, and after crossing the two branches of the Rigdikhola, ascended the side of a spur to the small village of *Kaolia*. Distance 3½ miles; road difficult, owing to ups and downs.

84. 26th December.—Continued up the side of the spur to another village named Kaolia, and proceeded thence along the crest to the fort of *Upardángarhi*. Distance 4 miles; road difficult. The fort is square with a side of 100 paces, and has masonry walls (loop-holed) rising to a height of about 25 feet. In the hot weather, the fort affords a sanatarium for between two and three hundred Nepalese soldiers who are sent up to it from the plains *iláka* of Chitaun. The party was closely interrogated here, and owing to the disturbed state of the country the explorer's arms (consisting of an old double-barrelled gun and four *kukris*) were taken away. After a detention of five days the party was allowed to proceed southwards.

85. 1st January 1886.—Proceeded by a stiff descent along the crest of a spur to Seriabás thána which was unoccupied at the time, and thence by a gentler slope to the flat jungle-land below; continued southwards to the hamlet of Dábarpáni* and beyond to that of *Kalwapur* on the right bank of a stream which rises east of Upardángarhi and falls into the Rápti. Distance 7 miles; road difficult, owing to dense undergrowth in the forest passed through.

86. 2nd January.—Proceeded about a couple of miles, and having lost the path (owing to dense jungle) returned to Kalwapur: having secured a guide, the party set out again and halted at the hamlet of *Gotholi*. Distance 3 miles; road as yesterday.

87. 3rd January.—Route turned westwards, and continued through dense undergrowth to *Parsoni*, a village of 15 or 20 houses and the residence of a Nepalese forest officer. Distance 1½ miles;

---

* From this village southwards, the inhabitants of the villages are Thárus an agricultural sect of lowlanders.

road as yesterday. As a convenient northerly track strikes away from Parsoni, the explorer himself halted at this village while he sent a man of his party (whom he had partially instructed in traversing) under pretence of bathing at the temple of Gaughát (situated in the angle formed at the junction of the Seti and Tirsúli rivers) to proceed thence down the river. A ferry-boat carries passengers across the Tirsúli both at Gaughát and Deoghát lower down. The man traversed down a fair road along the eastern bank of the river through the villages of Gethi and Dumra to opposite Deoghát temple situated at the confluence of the Káli Gunduk and the Tirsúli rivers, the volume of water in both rivers being said to be about equal. Below the confluence the river is known as the Naráini. At Deoghát an annual religious fair is held in the beginning of February. This fair lasts for about a month, and large quantities of goods as well as cattle and ponies change hands here. The traders who frequent the fair come all the way from Pokhra, Khatmandu, Batoli, and Bettiah, and heavy taxes are levied by the Nepalese Government on the goods brought for sale. Nearly two miles below Deoghát is the small village and chauki of Dhárigaon, and about three miles lower down is the large village and military post of Naráingarh where the man was joined by the explorer.

88. 8th January.—Left Parsoni and proceeded through dense jungle infested by wild elephants to Naráingarh. This is a place of some importance, being a depôt where all the timber floated down the river in winter is examined and duty levied. About 50 soldiers under the command of a *Subadár* are stationed here. The road beyond Naráingarh was found cut away by the river, and the party had to strike a path through the forest, after which not being able to recover the road they continued their way as best they could to the small village of *Phaleni.* Distance 8½ miles ; road very bad.

89. 9th January.—Owing to a belt of dense forest (chiefly of *Sissoo*) standing on the left bank of the Naráini river down to a couple of miles north of the junction with it of the Rápti, the road leaves the river and skirts the eastern edge of the forest. Passing through the small temporary hamlets of Bancharia, Belua, Langota, and Hatáhi, the party halted at the hamlet of *Simri.* Distance 6½ miles ; road fair.

90. 10th January.—Passed through the hamlets of Sisai and Sakarbhát (Ghágra and Dadarhani being at short distances off the road) to the large village of *Jítpura.* Distance 4½ miles ; road good. From here a good road leads south for Bettiah : the Rápti is said to be about 2 miles distant to the south.

91. 11th January.—Continued the route through Najagaon hamlet to Pathargaon village and chauki. The explorer's party was interrogated and their goods examined, when having declared themselves to be nothing more than pilgrims they were allowed to proceed. At about a mile beyond, the right bank of the Rápti was reached. This river has here a sandy bed about 400 paces across, with a sluggish current, the width of the channel being about 200 paces and the depth of water only about 2 feet. Having forded the river, the party halted on the left bank at about 2 miles lower down. Distance 6 miles ; road good.

92. 12th January.—At about a mile lower down is Kuriaghát, at the junction of the Rápti and Naráini, and thence a view of the latter was obtained for about 2 miles higher up. The combined waters are said to form a river the water-channel of which is estimated to be about 500 paces wide. At Kuriaghát a ferry plies across the river. The route lay along the left bank for some 4 miles, at first through open ground and afterwards through jungle at the foot of the hills, till the Leraghát ferry was reached. After continuing along the bank for more than a mile further, the road leaves it to avoid a bend in the river, and entering the hills tops a long spur running east and west. The Kanha nadi at the base of the spur having been crossed, the party proceeded about a mile further, and halted at a spot where some men proceeding southwards with grain were found bivouacked. Distance 11 miles ; road difficult.

93. 13th January.—Continued through the broken hilly ground for about a mile southwards ; the route then struck off westwards for nearly 2 miles, after which it took a southwesterly turn and kept parallel to the river (at nearly three-quarters of a mile to the east) till the Pachnad stream was met. The party having forded the stream continued along its left bank to the sheds opposite *Tirbenighát.* Distance 5½ miles ; road difficult.

94. *Trade.*—The trade from the Lhása direction between Dingri and Khatmandu is chiefly carried over the Nilam Jong route a description of which will be found at page 3—, of the General Report of the Great Trigonometrical Survey for 1871-72. There is no trade whatever on the route between Dingri and Jongkhajong, but the latter forms a convenient *entrepôt* for the Dokpas and other Tibetan traders from the north and north-west, who in summer bring down salt, goats, blankets, muskpods, and ponies, for the Khatmandu market. As the Nilam Jong route is absolutely impracticable for ponies, the trade in these is very largely forced into the route *viâ* Jongkhajong and Kirong. The traders return with rice, tobacco-leaf, brass and copper vessels, and cotton and woollen cloths imported from India.

EXPLORATION REPORT ON ROUTES BY EXPLORER M——H.

95. The Nubri *iláka* is celebrated as the tract in which the plant the root of which is known as *Nirbisi* is indigenous. Large quantities of the root are gathered in the months of July to October, and after being dried in the shade are ready for export. The root is then chiefly exported north-wards and north-westwards, while a comparatively small quantity finds its way south. Besides this, a few skins of *munáls* and Argus pheasants are brought down for transport to the Indian market. It will thus be seen that the Búri Gunduk route is not utilized as a regular trade-route between Tibet and Nepal. On the banks of the Naráini, as far north as a little beyond Gaughát, quantities of *sál, toon,* and other timber are cut by men who go up for the purpose from British territory. The timber is floated down the river in log and large stacks of it are to be met at Tirbeni.

96. Of domestic animals, the only ones met with in the portion of Tibet between Dingri, Jong-khajong, and Rasiagarhi, are yáks, *zobus,* goats, and sheep, with a few fowls occasionally to be seen at the large places. In Nepal to about latitude $28\frac{1}{4}°$ along the route taken by the explorer, buffaloes, cows, and goats are every where met with; while further north the country is exclusively inhabited by Tibetans, and sustains yáks, *zobus,* and sheep.

97. *Fauna.* Besides a few Tibetan antelopes (*Antilopus Hodgsonii*) found in the open country west of Dingri, the only kinds of wild animals seen by the explorer were the golden wolf of Tibet (*Lupus chanco*), the marmot (*Arctomys bombae*) and the rat-hare or tailless rat (*Lagomys*), but of this last he is unable to furnish any description which would serve to identify the particular species that was met with. Tigers and elephants abound in the dense *sál* jungles which stretch away east of the Naráini below Gaughát.

98. *Flora.* Between Dingri and Tashirák (about $10\frac{1}{2}$ miles south of Jongkhajong) not a tree of any kind is to be seen. There is, however, abundance of grass and furze to be met with all along the route. At Tashirák no furze was seen, but a few stunted willows (? *Salix Lindleyana*) and a species of barberry (*Berberis aristata* called *Chotra* by the natives) were met on the river sides as far south as Gunda. From Gunda to a little below Kirong dense forests of the *Abies Webbiana* are met with at the lower elevations, and of the *Betula bhojpattra* on the higher mountain-sides, with a thick undergrowth of the mountain-bamboo or *ringál.* Specimens of the creeping-cedar or juniper shrub (? *Juniperus religiosa* called *bil* by the Nepalese and used by the Tibetans as an incense) and of the red currant (*hisálu* of the Nepalese) were also met with. As is to be noticed in other parts of the Himalayas, the northern faces of the mountains were generally found to be more luxuriant both in arboreous and shrubby vegetation, due partly to greater depth of soil and partly to less direct influence of solar rays. From Thungsia (a little below Kirong) to a couple of miles beyond Rámcha—practically the middle belt of Himalayan vegetation, *i.e.,* from about 5 to 9000 feet in elevation—the arboreous specimens of temperate climes were found to flourish. These were, the common oak (*Quercus incana*), rhododendron *arboreum,* wild cherry (*Cerasus padam*), the mountain pear (? *Pyrus variolosa* or *lanata*), and a tree known by the natives under the name of *Añyár* (most probably the *Andromeda ovalifolia*) the young leaves of which secrete a viscous fluid in March and April and are then poisonous if eaten by cattle but not so later on when the leaves are fully de-veloped. It is said that honey extracted from the flowers of this tree (which blossoms luxuriantly every three years) is also possessed of somewhat deleterious properties, and is therefore not used by the hill people: in this last quality it corresponds with *Kalmia latifolia* one of the Rhodoreæ. A dense undergrowth of a thinner species of *ringál* is to be met with all along this part of the route.

99. South from Rámcha to Naiakot, thence westwards to Arughát, and northwards again to Lodánda, the usual tropical specimens met with in the lowest belt of Himalayan vegetation were seen, such as mangoes, plantains, the large bamboo, jackfruit, *semal, toon, sissoo* (*Dalbergia sissoo*), with some dwarfed *sál* trees. Beyond Lodánda and as far north as Niák, vegetation appertaining to the middle belt was met, but not so uniformly dense as between Gunda and Kirong: still further north *Abies Webbiana, Quercus dilatata* and *semecarpifolia* (the latter called *khursoo* by the Nepalese), *Betula bhojpattra* (which attains the highest elevation) with an undergrowth of *ringál* jungle were to be seen for some distance up the mountain-sides. Neither furze, juniper, nor rhododendrons of any kind were noticed; though there can be little doubt that the two latter must exist at the higher limits. In the portion of the Nubri *iláka* north of Pángsing, *Aconitum heterophyllum* (the *atees* of the Natives and highly valued for its medicinal properties) is found. The root of this plant is said to be of an ashy color with two fusiform tubers very white inside and of a bitter taste, thus corresponding exactly with the description given by Royle: the roots are gathered from June to December and dried in the shade. Another plant of the same kind called *bis* is also met with in this locality: this is probably the *Aconitum ferox,* and is described by the explorer as differing from the *atees* in the following essentials, *viz.,* that the plant sends up *several* stalks emanating from *several* yellowish-white tubers congregated round the root, (while the *atees* has but a single stalk); the tubers are also much larger than those of the *atees,* and they do not acquire a proper consistency till November and December. The root, though highly poisonous, is used medicinally for rheumatism and other diseases: for this purpose it is encased in a thick covering of cow-dung and well baked so as to reduce the virulence of its poison. Owing to its

deadly properties, and the improper uses to which it had been put, the Nepalese Government have issued stringent orders against any trade being carried on in it. But the most important plant found in this locality is the famous *Nirbisi* of the natives which is said to be—as its name signifies—an antidote to poison. As its specific identification was, and perhaps still is, a matter of considerable doubt, it is much to be regretted that the explorer did not actually see the plant. From accounts that he heard, he says it has only a single stalk; the leaves are long-petioled, lobed, and crenated, and occur only at the base: the stalk rises to a height of about 1½ feet and the inflorescence is about as copious as in the *atees*: the peduncles spring from small white sessile bracts, and support more than one flower: the flower is of the same color as that of the *atees*, with one of the petals somewhat caudated. The root has two or three tubers from 1 to 2½ inches in length. The tubers brought down by the explorer are generally cuneiform, the heart being white, or brown; but he avers that in some few the heart is of a *reddish colour*, and these are much more valuable than the others.

List of Vernacular (Nepalese and Tibetan) words, with their signification or equivalent.

Nepalese.				Tibetan.			Signification or Equivalent.
Añyár	...	...				...	The *Andromeda ovalifolia*.
Atees	...	...				...	The *Aconitum heterophyllum*.
Bazár	...	...	(Háta)		...	...	Market.
			Bhanjang		...	...	Mountain-range of contracted extent.
Bhansár	...				...		Chief custom-house.
Biási	...	...				...	Winter-residence; see also *Phedi* (*N*).
Bil	...	...				...	The creeping-cedar, or *Juniperus religiosa*.
Bis	...	...				...	The *Aconitum ferox*.
			Chángbo		...	...	River; see also *Sángpo* (*T.*) and *Kosi* (*N*).
			Chánko		...	...	The Tibetan wolf of a greyish-yellow colour (*Lupus chanco*).
Chauki	...	...					Custom-house or police station.
	...		Chho		...	...	Lake; see also *Pokhri* and *Kund* (*N*).
	...		Chhu		...	...	Stream; see also *Khola* (*N*).
(Tátapáni)	...	...	Chhuchhán		...	...	A hot spring.
	...		Cho		...	...	The Tibetan antelope (*Antilopus Hodgsonii*).
Chotra	...						A species of barberry (*Berberis aristata*), from decocting the bark and wood of which the best kind of the native medicine *rasot* is obtained.
	...		Chungja		...	...	A middling quality of tea.
	...		Daibung		...	...	Governor of a province.
(Jhaukando)	...		Dáma		...	...	Tibetan furze (*Caragana Gerardiana, Caragana versicolor,* and a species of *Astragalus*).
Deodiár (or Diár)	...						The *Pinus deodara*.
Dhunga	...	...	(Dhoa)		...	...	Stone; whence Dhunga-Sángún (*N*) a stone bridge.
	...		Dok		...	...	A black tent.
	...		Dokpa		...	...	Literally a dweller in black tents; a nomad.
Dúdhkund	...	...	Hunúchho		...	...	Milky lake.
(Pola)	...	...	Dum (or Dámu)		...	...	A brick of tea.
Gaon	...	...	(Dong, Dongba, Lungba)			...	Village.
Garhi	...	...	(Khar)		...	...	Fort or fortress.
	...		Ghangár		...	...	A plain of some extent; see also *Thanka* (*T.*)
Ghát	...	...	(Rab or Raph)		...	...	A river-crossing, whether by ford, ferry, or bridge.
	...		Gonpa		...	...	A lamasery.
Gurral	...	...					The Himalayan chamois (*Nemorhædus goral*).
	...		Gyángpa		...	...	Chief village official.
	...		Gyatiu		...	...	A riding-mule.
Hisálu	...	...				...	The red currant (*Ribes*).
Iláka	...	...				...	District.
	...		Jong		...	...	Residence (whether a fort or otherwise) of a governor of a district who is called *Jongpon*.
	...		Jungchhongpan			...	Title of a *commercial* representative of the Lhása Government.
Khark	...	...	Dhong		...	...	Cattle-sheds.
	...		Khatág		...	...	A small silken handkerchief, bestowed either as an offering or as a mark of favour.
Khola	...	...	Chhu		...	...	Stream.
Khursoo	...	...				...	A species of oak (*Quercus semecarpifolia*).
Kosi	...	...	Chángbo (or Sángpo)			...	River.
Kukri	...	...					The short, heavy, curved knife used throughout Nepal in place of a sword.
Kund	...	...	Chho		...	...	Lake.
	...		Kyáng		...	...	The wild horse (*Equus hemionus* or *kyang*).
	...		Lá		...	...	Pass over a mountain range.
	...		Libún		...	...	A species of turnip.
Maidán	...	...	Ghangár or Thanka			...	A plain of some extent.
Munál	...	...					A species of pheasant (*Lophophorus Impeyanus*).
	...		Naktáng		...	...	A Tibetan coin (of equal parts of silver and alloy) valued at a half-rupee.
	...		Neh		...	...	A species of barley.

NOTE.—Words in the first and second columns which are enclosed in ( ) do not occur in the Report.

List of Vernacular (Nepalese and Tibetan) words.—(Continued).

Nepalese.			Tibetan.		Signification or Equivalent.
Newár	...	...		...	The trading sect in Nepal.
Nirbisi	...	...		...	Literally poison-antidote; a plant of the Aconite species.
Pahár	...	...	(Rhi)	... ...	Hill or mountain.
Patti	...	...		...	A fiscal division of territory, subordinate to a native revenue-collector.
Pawa	...	...	(Kunkháng)	... ...	Charitable rest-house (*Dharmsála* in Hindi).
Phedi	...	...		...	Winter residence.
Pokhri	...	...	Chho	... ...	*Small* lake.
Rasia	...	...	(Chhiák)	... ...	Boundary.
Ráíndiár	...	...		...	The most magnificent species of pine (*Abies Webbiana*), the foliage of which is arranged in the form of a cone.
Riáns	...	...		...	A species of oak (*Quercus dilatata*).
Sáñgúñ	...	...	(Shamba)	... ...	Bridge.
	...		Táma	... ...	A species of pea.
Tár	...			...	Level land bordering a river, whether cultivated or waste.
(Hulák)	...	...	Tarjum	... ...	Post-house, or official staging-place.
Thána	...	...		...	Police-station.
	...		Thanka	... ...	A plain of some extent.
Thár	...	...		...	The Himalayan wild-goat (*Hemitragus Jemblaicus*).
	...		Tíu	... ...	A burthen-mule.
	...		Zobu	... ...	Cross breed (male) between yák and cow.
	...		Zomu	.. ...	Cross breed (female) between yák and cow.

NOTE.—Words in the first and second columns which are enclosed in ( ) do not occur in the Report.

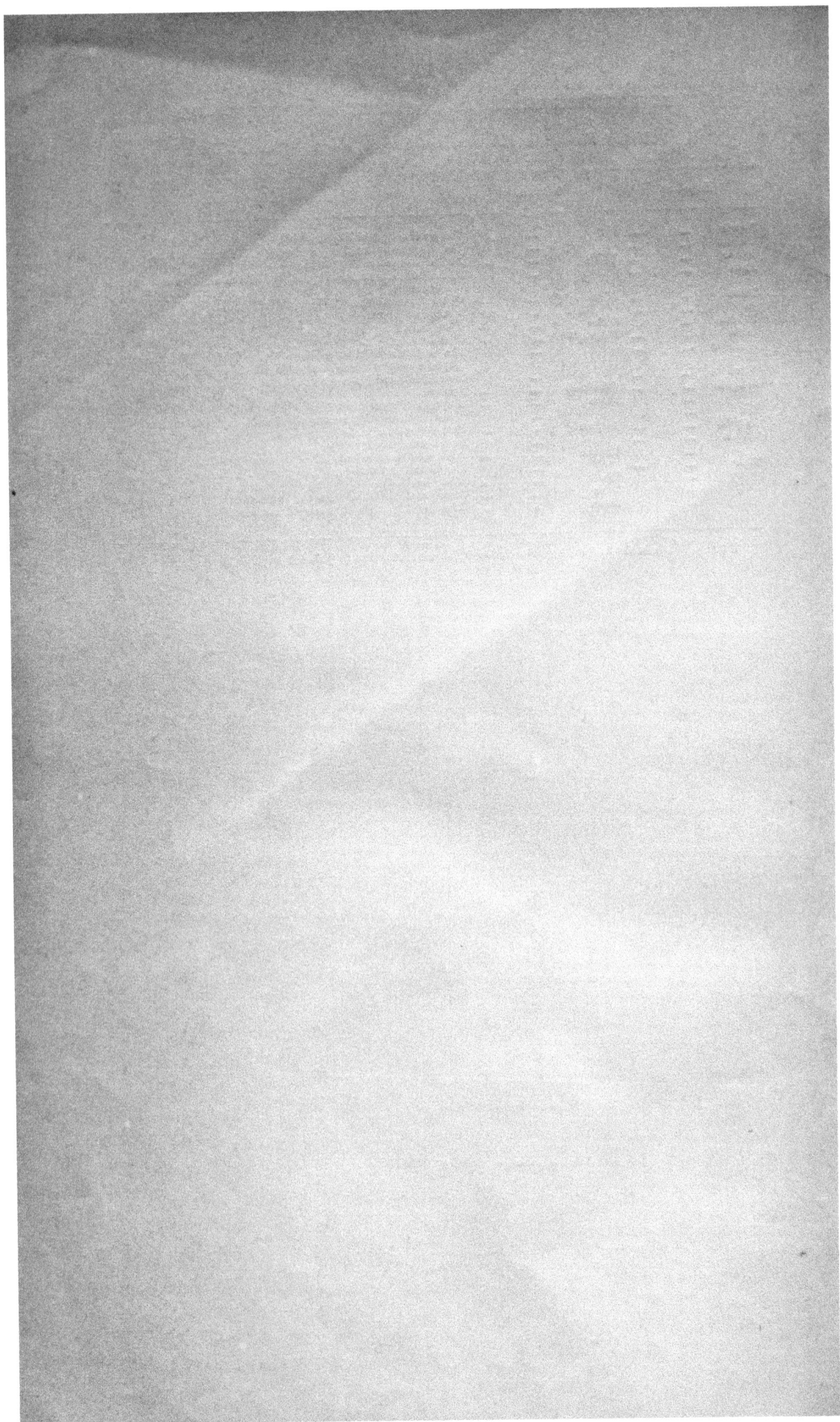

SKETCH MAP

ILLUSTRATING THE ROUTE OF
EXPLORER M—H

From Dagmara thana via the Dudhkosi to Dingri, and thence via
Jongkhajong and Kirong to Tirbenighat.

Season 1885-86.

Scale 1 Inch = 16 Miles or $\frac{1}{1013760}$

Scale of Miles

This map has been constructed on the following basis :—

(a). The positions of Dagmara thána, the gorge of the Khombu Changlu immediately above its junction with the Dudh Kosi between Snowy Peaks XVI and XVII, Tirbenighat, and Dingri, as furnished by the survey along the Nepal frontier executed under Colonel Tanner.

(b). The position values (lat. 27° 42' 0", long. 85° 21' 18") for Khatmandu Pillar, as determined by observations taken in 1884 by Lieut.-Colonel A. Wilson, Resident in Nepal.

(c). The latitude of Dingri (28° 25') astronomically determined by Explorer M—H in 1871-72, and the longitude (86° 44' 60") as furnished by that Explorer's route from Khatmandu to Shigatse adjusted between the above quoted longitude of Khatmandu and that of Shigatse taken as 88° 48' 30".

(d). The latitudes of Ramcha, Shabru, Rasuagadi, and Kirong (28° 1' 52", 28° 6' 34", 28° 10' 30", 28° 27' 0") astronomically determined in 1885-86 by Explorer Naip Sing, and their longitudes (85° 17' 0", 85° 17' 20", 85° 25' 45", 85° 18' 12") as furnished by that Explorer's route from Khatmandu to Tadum adjusted for the above longitude of Khatmandu.

Note.—The position of Nilamjong is dependent on its latitude (28° 5') astronomically determined by Explorer M—H in 1871-72, and longitude furnished by that Explorer's route thence along the Bhotia Kosi river adjusted to the position assigned to that part of the river from Colonel Tanner's trigonometrical determinations of several peaks on the two spurs between which it flows.

The delineation of the mountain features of the Himalaya, Mahábhárat, and Madhuria ranges has been derived from sketches by Colonel Tanner from the stations of the North-East Longitudinal Series bordering on the Nepal Frontier.

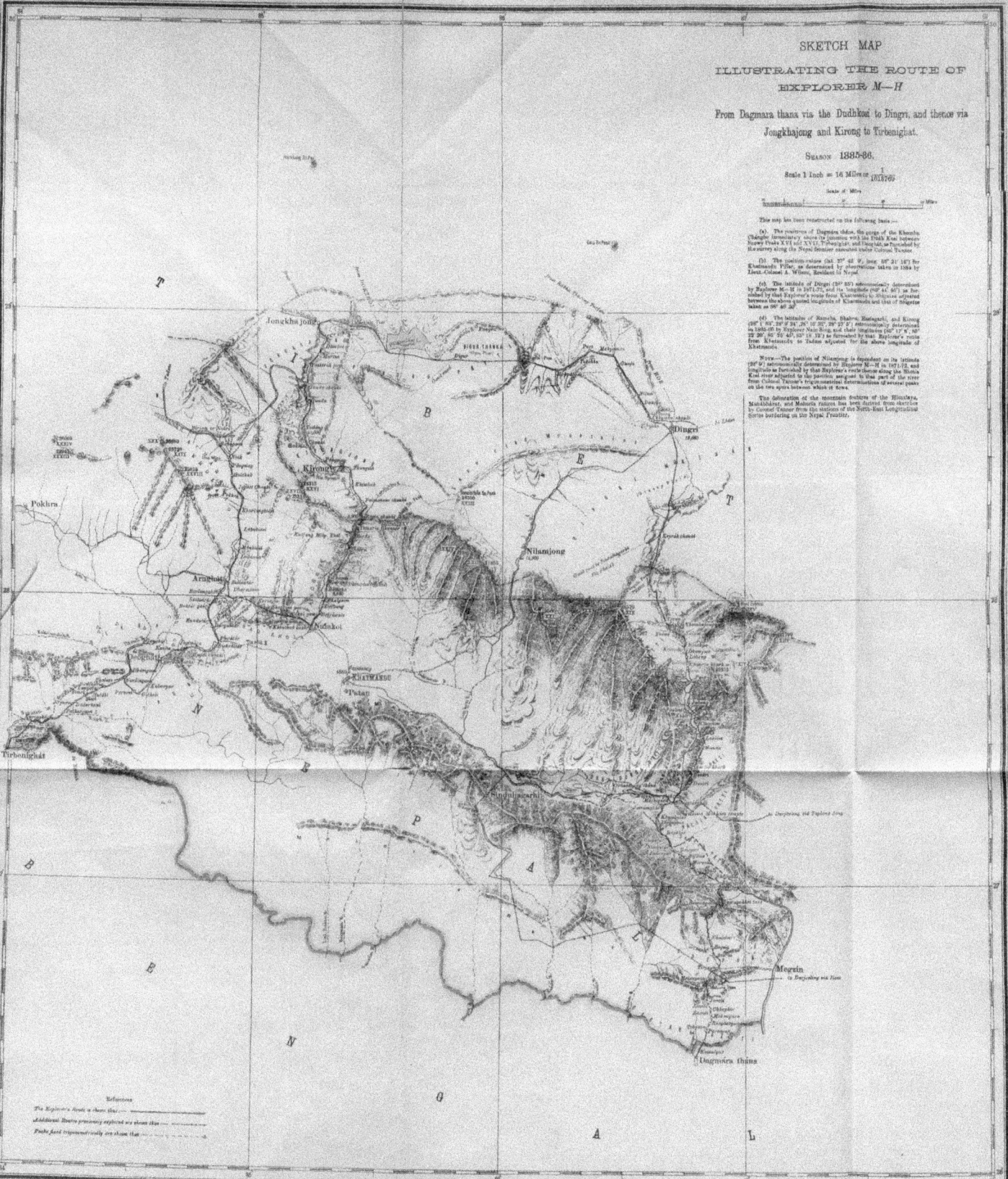

Jongkhajong

Dingri

Khonga

Pokhra

Nilamjong

Arughat

Nuakot

Chatmandu

Patati

Tirbenighat

Sindhulimarhi

Megzin
to Darjeeling via Rano

Dagmara thána

Compiled at the Office of the Trigonometrical Branch, Survey of India, Colonel G. C. Haig, R.E., Offg. Deputy Surveyor General in charge, and published under the direction of Lieut.-Colonel H. R. Thuillier, R.E., Offg. Surveyor General of India, April 1887.

Photozincographed at the Office of the Trigonometrical Branch, Dehra Dún, April 1887.